# HISTORIC
# Trades

*Colonial Williamsburg*

If you listen as you stroll the streets of Colonial Williamsburg's Revolutionary City, you hear the pulses of work—the whoosh of a sharp plane surfacing a board and the rustle of silk as a gown is sewn. Axes thump into wood; anvils ring to hammer strikes. Those sounds are the heartbeats of the Historic Trades program, a community of men and women at more than twenty sites, nearly one hundred masters and mistresses, journeymen and journeywomen, apprentices, and historic interpreters practicing eighteenth-century trades.

Tracing its beginnings to 1936, Colonial Williamsburg's Historic Trades program is the largest, most diverse museum-operated trades program in the world. Working in re-created eighteenth-century shops and using traditional techniques and tools to make reproductions of period products, the Foundation's artisans continue these trades as living occupations. Their range of knowledge and skills enables them to create almost any period product, from vehicles to clothing to guns to furniture. These men and women can construct a house from the ground up and furnish it—and its occupants—from top to bottom. In the process, they depict the lives of working men and women in early America. They also help us understand the importance of technology and why its changes impact our lives today.

The mission of the Historic Trades program encompasses four components:

## Presentation

Historic Trades is an important component of Colonial Williamsburg's educational programs. Tradespeople talk with and perform their work for hundreds of thousands of adults, children, and school groups each year. They present special programs in Williamsburg and across the nation.

## Preservation

Many trades practiced in Colonial Williamsburg's Historic Area no longer survive in their traditional forms anywhere else. The only way to preserve them is to pass them down from generation to generation. Today, as in the eighteenth century, individuals learn their trades by serving apprenticeships that last six or seven years. On completion, they achieve journeyman/woman status. A few become masters and mistresses, a recognition of their advanced knowledge, skills, teaching ability, and capability of running a shop.

## Discovery and Research

Historical accuracy in the Historic Trades program demands never-ending research. Tradespeople study historical documents related to their trades, those who practiced them, and the world in which they worked. They also study original eighteenth-century products, looking at the smallest details to determine how they were made and why their makers did things the way they did. This information becomes the basis for replicating products using historically accurate materials, tools, and techniques.

## Practice and Production

Achieving all of these goals depends on actually doing the work. Colonial Williamsburg's tradespeople practice their trades daily. The objects they make can be found throughout the Historic Area, at other historic sites, and in private collections. Some of their wares are offered for sale to the public through special orders and at the Prentis Store.

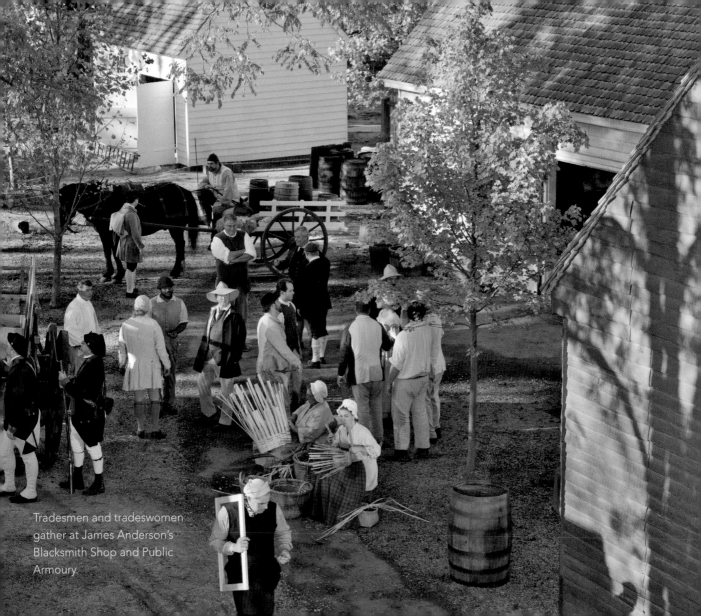

Tradesmen and tradeswomen gather at James Anderson's Blacksmith Shop and Public Armoury.

Double striking at the blacksmith's forge.
Work goes much faster with two.

Many products of the blacksmith require precision
fitting, filing, and finishing.

At the Geddy Foundry, founders use patterns to make molds of sand into which they pour molten brass. The castings require hours of assembly, refining, and polishing.

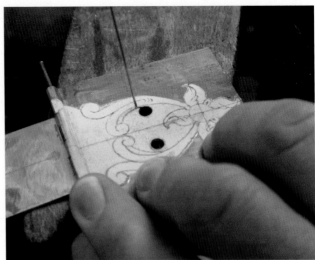

The gunsmith's trade requires the ability to work in wood and metals. Saw piercing a rifle's patch box finial and engraving a pistol's butt plate are two processes leading to a firearm's status as a decorative possession as well as utilitarian tool.

Oyster shells burned in a "rick" result in lime for mortar and plaster. Sun-dried bricks molded of clay are assembled into a "clamp." In the heat of the fire for days, they bake into sturdy building blocks.

A major portion of the carpenters' work is preparing materials, hewing logs into timbers, and sawing them into planks and "scantlings," or framing timbers. The materials are cut to size, and frames are assembled on the ground before being raised into their final positions.

While carpenters construct building frames and cover them with roofing and siding, joiners work at their benches to make windows, doors, moldings, and other trim. Some also prepare paints using natural pigments.

Hubs, spokes, and "fellies," the wooden outside rims of wheels, require careful shaping and fitting to withstand the strains of travel over rough roads.

Once the wooden parts are assembled, a heated iron tire is set onto the wheel and cooled with water. Cooling shrinks the tire and binds the whole wheel together.

Expensive carriages and utilitarian vehicles alike are painted and decorated according to their status.

Coopered containers are made of wooden staves and bound with metal hoops. Barrels and other casks are convenient for shipping and storing heavy material because they can be rolled easily from place to place.

Baskets, made by weaving together thin strips of split white oak, come in as many sizes and shapes as there are jobs for them to do.

Kitchen gardens supply households with fresh vegetables and herbs. Some go beyond the utilitarian, however, and are passionate about exotic vegetables, flowers, and fruits and the art of horticulture.

Small farms in the rural countryside produce tobacco as a cash crop and wheat and corn as both cash and subsistence crops.

When human effort is impractical, horses and oxen
can take up the load.

Wool from local sheep is cleaned, spun, dyed, and woven into yard goods for clothing and household items like bed hangings and blankets.

Fashion is never out of style. The mantua-maker cuts and fits a woman's gown directly over the customer in her stays. The milliner makes and sells a host of fashion accessories, available ready- and custom-made.

Tailors make men's suits and women's riding habits. Paper tapes are snipped at various points to record measurements. They traditionally sew sitting cross-legged on a tailor's board in front of a window for good light.

Shoes can be purchased ready-made or custom ordered. The master cuts the leather components to shape and size and passes along the pieces to his workmen for assembly and finishing.

Military artificers provide and maintain an army's many pieces of equipment. An artificer working in leather makes and cares for cartridge boxes, belts, scabbards, valises, saddles, and other accoutrements.

The wigmaker weaves strands of horse, yak, or human hair around rows of thread and sews the rows to a cap-like "caul." The wig, a mark of status and an important facet of men's dress, is then fashioned to the customer's taste.

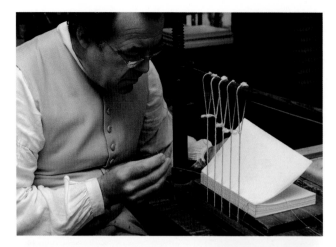

After beating the pages to make them lie flat and stitching them together, the bookbinder covers the book. Bindings range from the simplest paste paper to fine leather elaborately tooled, stamped, and decorated with designs sometimes rendered in gold leaf.

The printer sets each letter, locks the set type into a "chase," applies ink, and pulls the press by hand for each side of every sheet.

The shine of silver attracts the eye and conveys the wealth and status of its owner. Hollowware, such as bowls and cups, are hammered into shape from a flat sheet of silver. Silver is decorated with saw piercing, engraving, and three-dimensional chased and embossed designs.

The tin men at the Public Armoury produce a range of army camp items such as kettles, cups, plates, coffeepots, and small containers from tin-plated sheet iron. The items are lightweight, relatively quick to make, and inexpensive.

Cabinetmakers produce chairs, tables, chests of drawers, desks, and other pieces that are attractive yet, for the most part, "plain and neat" household furnishings.

Spinets and harpsichords are among of the most complex wooden mechanisms produced in town.

At the apothecary shop, mortars and pestles are used to crush items such as oyster shells for heartburn and cinchona bark for fevers. Delft drug storage jars line one wall. Copies of Dr. Galt's certificates in surgery and midwifery are on display.

Good food, from the governor's table to that of the soldier or field hand, is one of life's pleasures as well as its necessities. Professional cooks prepare elaborate dinners at the Governor's Palace while a hired hand bakes bread at the Public Armoury.

The publication of this book was made possible by a generous gift from Mr. and Mrs. Bruce M. Davidson of Annapolis, Maryland.

Photographs by David M. Doody and Tom Green

Additional photographs by Lael White and Barbara Temple Lombardi

25 24 23 22 21 20 19 18 17 16     2 3 4 5 6

Printed in the United States of America

ISBN 978-0-87935-266-0

Designed by Shanin Glenn

The Colonial Williamsburg Foundation is the not-for-profit center for history and citizenship.

Revolutionary City® and Colonial Williamsburg® are registered trade names of The Colonial Williamsburg Foundation.

The Colonial Williamsburg Foundation
Williamsburg, Virginia
colonialwilliamsburg.org